# EARTH NAMER

# EARTH

# NAMER

## A CALIFORNIA INDIAN MYTH RETOLD BY
## MARGERY BERNSTEIN & JANET KOBRIN
## ILLUSTRATED BY ED HEFFERNAN

CHARLES SCRIBNER'S SONS, NEW YORK

To
EDGAR BERNSTEIN
and
PHILIP MONTAG
whose talents created the Independent
Learning Project, and whose support and
enthusiasm made this book possible.

*Earth Namer* belongs to the Maidu Indians
of northern California.

IN the beginning of the world, there was water everywhere. There was no land.

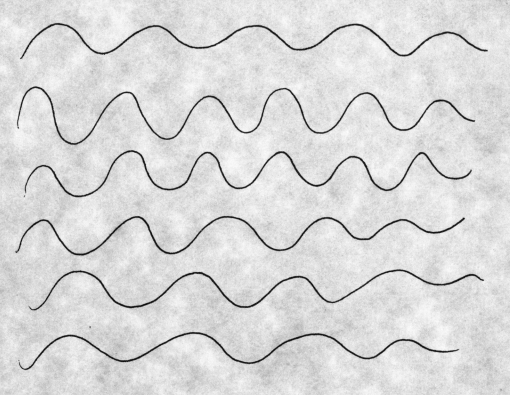

One day Turtle came floating along on a raft. No one knows where he came from.

As he floated along, a rope made of feathers dropped out of the sky.

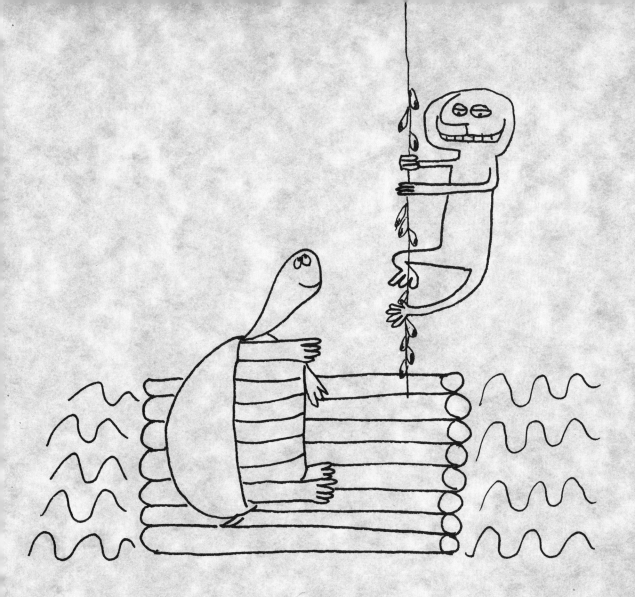

Turtle looked up and saw a man climbing
down the feather rope. The man climbed
down to the raft.

"Who are you?" asked Turtle. "What is your name?"

"My name is Earth Namer," said the man. Earth Namer sat down on the raft with Turtle.

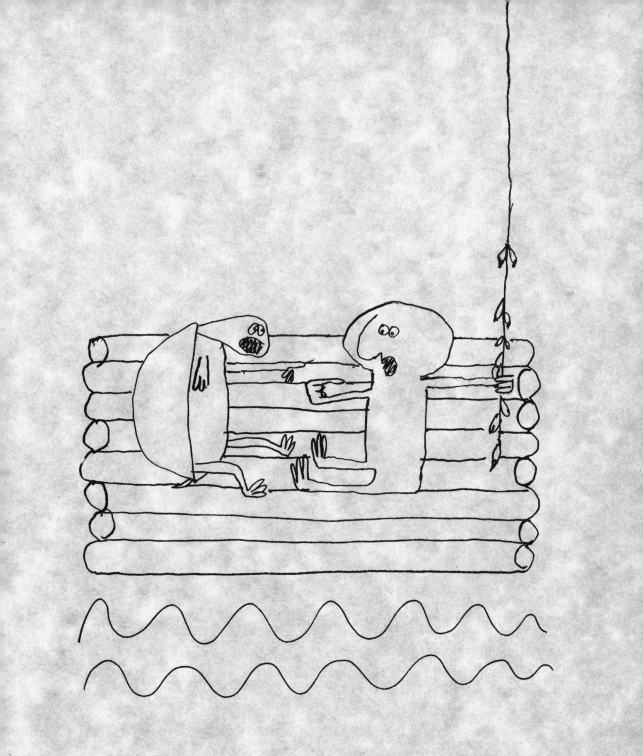

"Where are you from?" asked Turtle.

"From the sky," Earth Namer answered.

Then Turtle knew that Earth Namer must
be magic.

He decided to ask Earth Namer for a favor.

"Can you make dry land?" asked Turtle.
"I would like to rest."

Earth Namer thought for a while. "If you want me to make dry land, I must have a bit of earth," he said. "How can we get some?"

Turtle had an idea.

"If you will tie a rope to me, I will dive down to the bottom of the water. I will bring back some earth," he said.

So Earth Namer tied his feather rope to Turtle's leg.

Turtle dived down under the water.

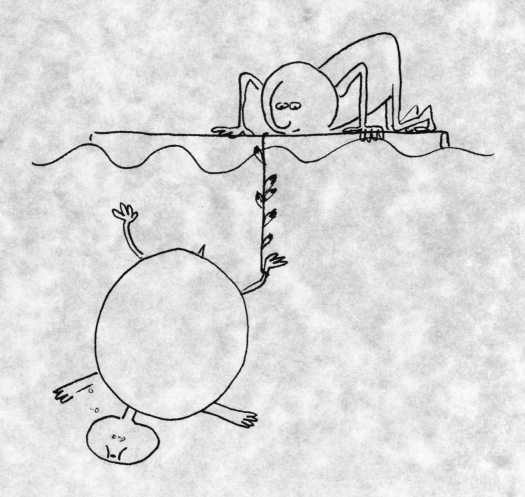

After a long time Turtle pulled on the
rope. Earth Namer helped him up to the
raft.

Turtle was very tired.

"Where is the earth?" Earth Namer asked.

"I have some under my fingernails," said Turtle.

Earth Namer took the bit of earth from
under Turtle's fingernails.

He rolled it into a ball. He put the ball
on the raft.

Then Earth Namer waited. Turtle waited
too.

Soon the ball of earth began to grow. First the ball was as big as Turtle.

And still it grew.

And then the ball was as big as the raft.
And still it grew.

It grew until it was as big as the world is now.

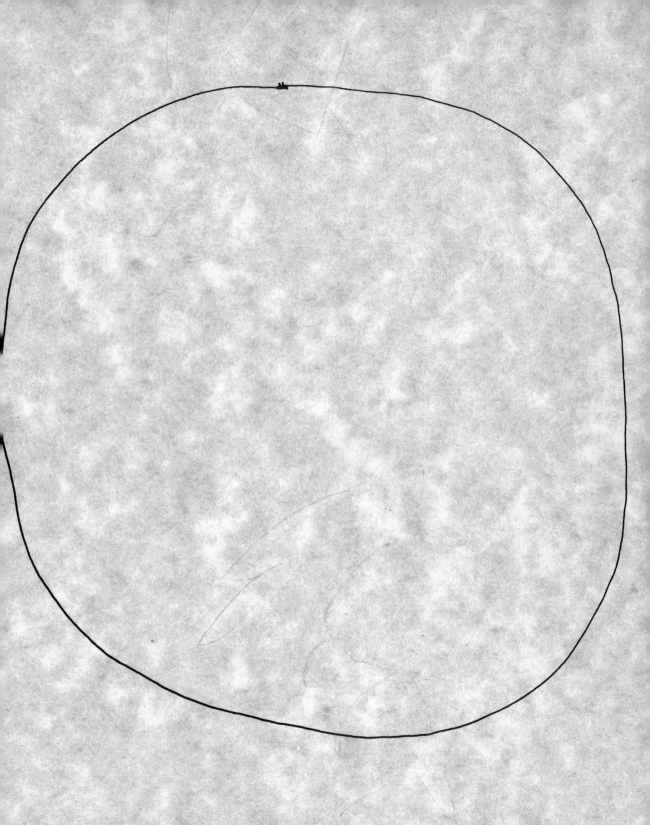

"We can get off the raft now," said Earth Namer. So they stepped onto the new land. But there was no light in this new land. It was very dark.

"We need light to see," said Turtle.

"Look there!" said Earth Namer. He
pointed to the east and the sun came up.
Then there was light and they could see.

Earth Namer showed the sun where to go
in the sky.

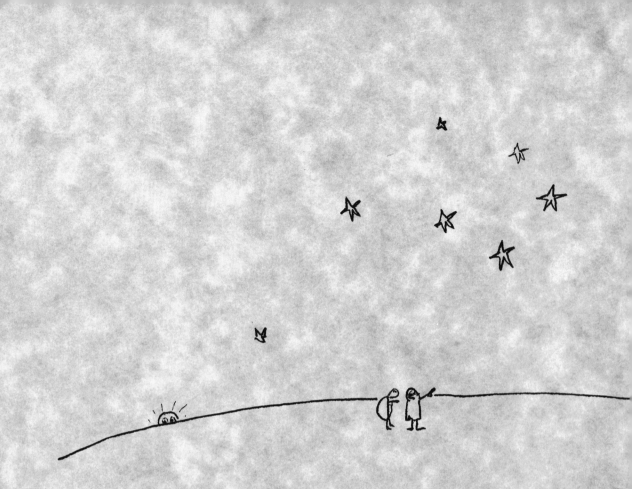

Then the sun went down and the moon
came up.

Earth Namer showed the moon where to
go.

28

Then he put the stars in the sky and gave
them names.

Earth Namer looked at the new land. He saw that it was empty.

So Earth Namer made trees and plants. He filled the earth with them.

Then he and Turtle rested in the shade.

After he had rested, Earth Namer made all the animals and birds.

Each of them went off to find homes in the new land.

Only Coyote stayed with Earth Namer and Turtle.

5

"Now it is time to make people to live on the land," Earth Namer said.

Earth Namer took some red-colored dirt. He mixed it with water. Very carefully, he shaped a man and a woman.

First Man and First Woman were very
beautiful. But their hands were not finished.
"How shall I make their hands?" asked
Earth Namer.

"Make their hands like mine so they can swim," said Turtle.

"Make their hands like mine so they can run fast," said Coyote.

Earth Namer thought and thought.

"No, they must have hands like mine.

They must have fingers so that they can make things," said Earth Namer.

Earth Namer made the hands of First Man
and First Woman to look like his own.

Then First Man and First Woman were
even more beautiful. They could do many
things the animals could not do.

First Man and First Woman thanked Earth
Namer.

All the animals and people stayed on the earth to live. Coyote and Turtle made their homes on the new land, too.

Only Earth Namer went away. He climbed up his feather rope, back to the sky.

He has never returned to earth again.